○

Axe Handles

POEMS BY

Gary Snyder

○

NORTH POINT PRESS
San Francisco
1983

Several of the poems in this collection first appeared, sometimes in somewhat different form, in the following periodicals, journals, broadsides, or chapbooks, to which the author and the publisher wish to express their thanks: *Field* ("Axe Handles," "Old Rotting Tree Trunk Down"), *Plucked Chicken* ("River in the Valley," "Under the Sign of Toki's"), *Copper Canyon* ("Among" [under the title "Yo' Mama"], "across salt marshes," "The manzanita," "as the crickets," "the stylishness," "Hear bucks skirmishing," deep blue sea, baby," "24:IV:75"), Bob Giorgio ("On Top" [under the title "A Mind Like Compost"], "True Night'), *New Directions Anthology 35* ("Berry Territory,'"), *Ohio Review* ("Bows to Drouth," "Walked Two Days," "Talking Late with the Governor"), *Kuksu 4* ("Painting the North San Juan School," "Working on the '58 Willys Pickup") *Kuksu 5* ("For All," "Money Goes Upstream"), *Kuksu 6* ("The Cool Around the Fire," "Fence Posts"), *Upriver Downriver 6* ("Look Back"), *Snapdragon* ("Soy Sauce"), *River Styx* ("Beetle Trails"), *Two Magpies Press* ("Awakened by the clock" [under the title "When to Not"], *Grindstone Press* ("hers"), *Sulfur* ("hers," "Uluru Wild Fig Song"), *Contact 2* ("I am sorry I disturbed you," "Old Woman Nature"), *The New York Times Sunday Magazine* ("The Grand Entry"), *Bastard Angel* "What Have I Learned"), *Mind, Moon Circle* ("Uluru Wild Fig Song").

Cover design: David Bullen
The cover painting, "Treasure Ship, Goddess of Snow," is from *Goddesses* by Mayumi Oda, published in 1981 by Lancaster Miller and Schnobrich, Berkeley, California.

North Point Press
850 Talbot Avenue
Berkeley, California
94706

This book is for San Juan Ridge

Table of Contents

How do you shape an axe handle?
Without an axe it can't be done.
How do you take a wife?
Without a go-between you can't get one.
Shape a handle, shape a handle,
the pattern is not far off.
And here's a girl I know,
The wine and food in rows.

From *Book of Songs* (*Shih Ching*)
(Mao no. 158): A folk song from
the Pin area, 5th C. B.C.

Axe Handles

PART ONE

Loops

○

Axe Handles

One afternoon the last week in April
Showing Kai how to throw a hatchet
One-half turn and it sticks in a stump.
He recalls the hatchet-head
Without a handle, in the shop
And go gets it, and wants it for his own.
A broken-off axe handle behind the door
Is long enough for a hatchet,
We cut it to length and take it
With the hatchet head
And working hatchet, to the wood block.
There I begin to shape the old handle
With the hatchet, and the phrase
First learned from Ezra Pound
Rings in my ears!
"When making an axe handle
          the pattern is not far off."
And I say this to Kai
"Look: We'll shape the handle
By checking the handle
Of the axe we cut with—"
And he sees. And I hear it again:

It's in Lu Ji's *Wên Fu*, fourth century
A.D. "Essay on Literature"—in the
Preface: "In making the handle
Of an axe
By cutting wood with an axe
The model is indeed near at hand."
My teacher Shih-hsiang Chen
Translated that and taught it years ago
And I see: Pound was an axe,
Chen was an axe, I am an axe
And my son a handle, soon
To be shaping again, model
And tool, craft of culture,
How we go on.

o

For/From Lew

Lew Welch just turned up one day,
  live as you and me. "Damn, Lew" I said,
"you didn't shoot yourself after all."
"Yes I did" he said,
  and even then I felt the tingling down my back.
"Yes you did, too" I said—"I can feel it now."
"Yeah" he said,
"There's a basic fear between your world and
  mine. I don't know why.
  What I came to say was,
  teach the children about the cycles.
  The life cycles. All the other cycles.
  That's what it's all about, and it's all forgot."

○

River in the Valley

We cross the Sacramento River at Colusa
follow the road on the levee south and east
find thousands of swallows nesting
on the underside of a concrete overhead
roadway? causeway? abandoned. Near
                    Butte Creek.

  Gen runs in little circles looking up
  at swoops of swallows—laughing—
                    they keep
  flowing under the bridge and out,

  Kai leans silent against a concrete pier
  tries to hold with his eyes the course
  of a single darting bird,

  I pick grass seeds from my socks.

The coast range. Parched yellow front hills,
blue-gray thornbrush higher hills behind,
and here is the Great Central Valley,

drained, then planted and watered,
    thousand-foot deep soils
    thousand-acre orchards

    Sunday morning,
only one place serving breakfast
in Colusa, old river and tractor men
sipping milky coffee.

From north of Sutter Buttes
we see snow on Mt. Lassen
and the clear arc of the Sierra
south to the Desolation peaks.
One boy asks, "where do rivers start?"

in threads in hills, and gather down to here—
but the river
is all of it everywhere,
all flowing at once,
all one place.

o

Among

Few Douglas fir grow in these pine woods
One fir is there among south-facing Ponderosa Pine,

Every fall a lot of little seedlings sprout
                                    around it—

Every summer during long dry drouth they die.
Once every forty years or so
A rain comes in July.

Two summers back it did that,
The Doug fir seedlings lived that year

The next year it was dry,
A few fir made it through.
This year, with roots down deep, two live.
A Douglas fir will be among these pines.

> *at the 3000-foot level*
> *north of the south fork*
> *of the Yuba river.*

o

On Top

All this new stuff goes on top
turn it over   turn it over
wait   and water down.
From the dark bottom
turn it inside out
let it spread through, sift down,
even.
Watch it sprout.

A mind like compost.

o

Berry Territory

(Walking the woods on an early spring dry
day, the slopes behind Lanes Landing Farm
on the Kentucky River, with Tanya and Wendell)

Under dead leaves Tanya finds a tortoise
    matching the leaves—legs pulled in—

And we look at woodchuck holes that dive
    under limestone ledges
    seabottom strata,
    who lives there brushes furry back
    on shell and coral,

Most holes with leaves and twigs around the door,
    nobody in.

Wendell, crouched down,
    sticks his face in a woodchuck hole
    "Hey, smell that, it's a fox!"
    I go on my knees,
    put the opening to my face
    like a mask. No light;
    all smell: sour—warm—

Splintered bones, scats? feathers?
Wreathing bodies—wild—

Some home.

○

Bows to Drouth

Driest summer,
The hose snakes under the mulch
    to the base of a gravenstein apple
    three years old,
And back to the standpipe
    where it dives underground.

At the pump,
    the handle extended with pipe
    sweeps down
    six strokes to a gallon,
    one hundred and fifteen feet deep
    force pump, the cylinder set in the water
Sucker-rod faintly clangs in the well.

Legs planted,
    both hands on the handle,
    whole body bending,
    I gaze through the trees and
    see different birds,
    different leaves,
    with each bow.

No counting,
     all free—
     deep water softly lifts out—
     over there—
At the base of an apple.

Drouth of the summer of '74

○

The Cool Around the Fire

Drink black coffee from a thermos
      sitting on a stump.

      piles burn down, the green limb
      fringe edge
      picked up and tossed in
To the center: white ash mound
      shimmering red within.
      tip head down
      to shield face
      with hat brim   from the heat;

The thinning, pruning, brush-cut
      robbed from bugs and fungus—
      belly gray clouds
      swing low soft over
      maybe rain, bring an end
      to this drouth;

Burn brush to take heat
     from next summer's wildfires
     and to bring rain on time,
     and fires clear the tangle.

     the tangle of the heart.
Black coffee, bitter, hot,
     smoke rises straight and calm
     air
Still and cool.

Changing Diapers

How intelligent he looks!
   on his back
   both feet caught in my one hand
   his glance set sideways,
   on a giant poster of Geronimo
   with a Sharp's repeating rifle by his knee.

I open, wipe, he doesn't even notice
   nor do I.
Baby legs and knees
   toes like little peas
   little wrinkles, good-to-eat,
   eyes bright, shiny ears,
   chest swelling drawing air,

No trouble, friend,
   you and me and Geronimo
   are men.

○

Beating the Average

Odd rain in August,
    Gen with asthma in the night kept us awake
    entered our bed, wheezing,
    scratching poison oak—

So tired today.
All morning down at Rod's and help
    adjust the valves,
    fix the back trunk lock.
More rain.

Zucchini recipes from Patty,
    and back home now,
    nap, try to forget,
    get head ready for state work tomorrow,
    fly early to L.A.,
    Arts Council meet.

Half asleep on the top bunk
        thinking of mushrooms that this rain will bring.
And the two boys five and seven
        race around the house
        shrieking, laughing, weeping, wailing,

        calls of kids
        echoing through the woods:
        calls of play.

The weather record says for August,
        0.000
        is the average rainfall here.

Painting the North San Juan School

White paint splotches on blue head bandanas
Dusty transistor with wired-on antenna
    plays sixties rock and roll;
Little kids came with us are on teeter-totters
    tilting under shade of oak
This building good for ten years more.
The shingled bell-cupola trembles
    at every log truck rolling by—

The radio speaks:
    today it will be one hundred degrees in the valley.
—Franquette walnuts grafted on the
    local native rootstock do o.k.
    nursery stock of cherry all has fungus;
Lucky if a bare-root planting lives,

This paint thins with water.
This year the busses will run only
    on paved roads,
Somehow the children will be taught:
How to record their mother tongue
    with written signs,

Names to call the landscape of the continent
                          they live on
Assigned it by the ruling people of the last
      three hundred years,
The games of numbers,
What went before, as told by those who
      think they know it,

A drunken man with chestnut mustache
Stumbles off the road to ask if he can help.

Children drinking chocolate milk

Ladders resting on the shaky porch.

o

All in the Family

For the first time in memory
heavy rain in August
   tuning up the chainsaw
      begin to cut oak
Boletus by the dozen
   fruiting in the woods
Full moon, warm nights
   the boys learn to float
Masa gone off dancing
   for another thirty days
Queen Anne's Lace in the meadow
   a Flicker's single call

Oregano, lavender, the *salvia* sage
   wild pennyroyal
   from the Yuba River bank
All in the family
   of Mint.

o

Fence Posts

It might be that horses would be useful
On a snowy morning to take the trail
Down the ridge to visit Steve or Mike and
Faster than going around the gravelled road by car.

So the thought came to fence a part of the forest,
Thin trees and clear the brush,
Ron splits cedar rails and fenceposts
On Black Sands Placer road where he gets
These great old butt logs from the Camptonville sawmill
Why they can't use them I don't know—
They aren't all pecky.
He delivers, too, in a bread van
His grandfather drove in Seattle.

Sapwood posts are a little bit cheaper than heartwood.
I could have bought all heartwood from the start
But then I thought how it doesn't work
To always make a point of getting the best which is why
I sometimes pick out the worse and damaged looking fruit
And vegetables at the market because I know

I actually will enjoy them in any case but
Some people might take them as second choice
And feel sour about it all evening.

With sapwood fenceposts
You ought to soak to make sure they won't rot
In a fifty-five gallon drum with penta 10 to 1
Which is ten gallons of oil and a gallon of
Termite and fungus poison.
I use old crankcase oil to dilute
And that's a good thing to do with it but,
There's not really enough old crank to go around.
The posts should be two feet in the ground.

So, soaking six posts a week at a time
The soaked pile getting bigger week by week,
But the oil only comes up one and a half feet.
I could add kerosene in
At seventy cents a gallon
Which is what it costs when you buy it by the drum
And that's $3.50 to raise the soaking level up
Plus a half a can of penta more, six dollars,
For a hundred and twenty fence posts
On which I saved thirty dollars by getting the sapwood,
But still you have to count your time,

A well-done fence is beautiful.
And horses, too.
Penny wise pound foolish either way.

Spring, '77

○

So Old—

Oregon Creek reaches far back into the hills.
Burned over twice, the pines are returning again.
Old roads twist deep into canyons,
    hours from one ridge to the next
The new road goes straight on the side of the mountain,
    high, and with curves ironed out.
A single hawk flies leisurely up,
    disturbed by our truck
Down the middle fork-south fork opening,
    fog silver gleams in the valley.
Camptonville houses are old and small,
    a sunny perch on a ridge,
Was it gold or logs brought people to this spot?
    a teenage mother with her baby stands by a pickup.
A stuffed life-size doll of a Santa Claus
    climbs over a porch-rail.
Our old truck too, slow down the street,
    out of the past—
It's all so old—the hawk, the houses, the trucks,
    the view of the fog—
Midwinter late sun flashes through hilltops and trees
    a good day, we know one more part of our watershed,

And have seen a gorge with a hairpin bend
    and followed one more dirt road to its end.
Chilling, so put on jackets
    and take the paved road out
Back to our own dirt road, iron stove,
    and the chickens to close in the dusk.
And the nightly stroll of raccoons.

○

Look Back

Twice one summer
I walked up Piute mountain,
our trailcrew was camped at Bear Valley.
I first had chainsaw practice
cutting wood there for the cook.
Piute mountain. And scanned the crest
of the Sawtooths, to the east.
A Whitebark pine relict stand
cut off from friends
by miles of air and granite—me
running out ridges.
Jimmy Jones the cook said "I
used to do that, run the ridges
all day long—just like a coyote."
When I built a little sweatlodge
one Sunday by the creek
he told me to be careful,
and almost came in too.

Today at Slide Peak in the Sawtooths
I look back at that mountain
twenty-five years. Those days
when I lived and thought all alone.

I was studying Chinese
preparing for Asia
every night after trail crew work
                                    from a book.
Jimmy Jones was a Mariposa Indian.
One night by the campfire
drinking that coffee black
he stood there looking down at my
H. G. Creel, "Those letters Chinese?"
"Yes," I said. He said, "Hmmmmm.
My grandpa they say was Chinese."

And that year I quit early.
told the foreman I was headed for Japan.
He looked like he knew, and said "Bechtel."
I couldn't tell him something strange as Zen.

Jimmy Jones, and these mountains and creeks.
The up and down of it
stays in my feet.

VII, '78, The Sawtooths.

Soy Sauce

for Bruce Boyd and Holly Tornheim

Standing on a stepladder
    up under hot ceiling
tacking on wire net for plaster,
a day's work helping Bruce and Holly on their house,
I catch a sour salt smell and come back
    down the ladder.

"Deer lick it nights" she says,
and shows me the frame of the window she's planing,
clear redwood, but dark, with a smell.

"Scored a broken-up, two-thousand-gallon redwood
soy sauce tank from a company went out of business
down near San Jose."

Out in the yard the staves are stacked:
I lean over, sniff them, ah! it's like Shinshu miso,
the darker saltier miso paste of the Nagano
uplands, central main island, Japan—
it's like Shinshu pickles!

I see in mind my friend Shimizu Yasushi and me,
one October years ago, trudging through days of snow
crossing the Japan Alps and descending
the last night, to a farmhouse,
taking a late hot bath in the dark—and eating
        a bowl of chill miso radish pickles,
        nothing ever so good!

Back here, hot summer sunshine dusty yard,
        hammer in hand.

But I know how it tastes
        to lick those window frames
        in the dark,
                    the deer.

○

Delicate Criss–crossing Beetle Trails
Left in the Sand

Masa's childhood village
the bus takes us through it again;

    soaked drooping bamboo groves
    swaying heavy in the drizzle,
    and perfectly straight lines of rice plants
    glittering orderly mirrors of water,
    dark grove of straight young Sugi trees
    thick at the base of the hill,

    a crow flaps, a
    cluster of yellow-hat children
    marching to kindergarten,
    right by the bus in the rain

Walking out on the beach, why I know this!
    rode down through those pines once
    with Anja and John

And watch bugs in their own tiny dunes.

from memory to memory,
bed to bed and meal to meal,
all on this road in the sand

Summer, '81, Tango, Japan Sea

Walking Through Myoshin-ji

Straight stone walks
   up lanes between mud walls

. . . the sailors who handled the ships
   from Korea and China,
the carpenters, chisels like razors,

   young monks working on *mu*,

   and the pine trees
     that surrounded this city.
     the Ancient Ones, each one
anonymous.
    green needles,
      lumber,
        ash.

VII, 81, Kyoto

○

Fishing Catching Nothing
off the Breakwater near the Airport,
Naha Harbor, Okinawa

Self-defense-force jets in pairs
scream out over the bay
lay a track of smoke and whine
on the Kumé islands

Clouds sailing right on the sea
clouds and waters
prairie of wavelets

Jet plane outriders—scouts—
Displaying with Soviet pilots
who's weak?   who's strong?

Burning millions of gallons of kerosene

Screaming along.

○

At the Ibaru Family Tomb
Tagami village, Great Loo Choo:
Grandfathers of my sons

Weeds in the stone courtyard
    stone door plastered shut,
    washed bones within
    ranked in urns,

We drink and sing in the courtyard:
    songs of a beautiful reef,
    songs of a grove
    they walked through long ago,

Drinking with the ancestors
    singing with their sons.

             VI, '81, Okinawa

○

Strategic Air Command

The hiss and flashing lights of a jet
Pass near Jupiter in Virgo.
He asks, how many satellites in the sky?
Does anyone know where they all are?
What are they doing, who watches them?

Frost settles on the sleeping bags.
The last embers of fire,
One more cup of tea,
At the edge of a high lake rimmed with snow.

These cliffs and the stars
Belong to the same universe.
This little air in between
Belongs to the twentieth century and its wars.

VIII, 82, Koip Peak, Sierra Nevada,

○

Eastward Across Texas

In a great cave of minerals and
    salts-in-shapes
Gen said he saw a Ringtail
    with a bat in its mouth

Out of mountains onto flat high land
    phosphate diggings,
And subtly down, eastward, dry wide plains
    till we come
    to a warm eve in Snyder, Texas.

Kai says to a waitress, "our name is Snyder too."
    She says, "Yeah, there's some Vietnamese
    refugees near here."
His black hair?

        obsidian in graves.

gifts to the future
    to remember us.

○

Working on the '58 Willys Pickup

For Lu Yu

The year this truck was made
I sat in early morning darkness
Chanting sūtra in Kyoto,
And spent the days studying Chinese.
Chinese, Japanese, Sanskrit, French—
Joys of Dharma-scholarship
And the splendid old temples—
But learned nothing of trucks.

Now to bring sawdust
Rotten and rich
From a sawmill abandoned when I was just born
Lost in the young fir and cedar
At Bloody Run Creek
So that clay in the garden
Can be broken and tempered
And growing plants mulched to save water—
And to also haul gravel
From the old placer diggings,
To screen it and mix in the sand with the clay
Putting pebbles aside to strew on the paths
So muddy in winter—

I lie in the dusty and broken bush
Under the pickup
Already thought to be old—
Admiring its solidness, square lines,
Thinking a truck like this
would please Chairman Mao.

The rear end rebuilt and put back
With new spider gears,
Brake cylinders cleaned, the brake drums
New-turned and new brake shoes,
Taught how to do this
By friends who themselves spent
Youth with the Classics—

The garden gets better, I
Laugh in the evening
To pick up Chinese
And read about farming,
I fix truck and lock eyebrows
With tough-handed men of the past.

○

Getting in the Wood

The sour smell,
　　blue stain,
　　　　water squirts out round the wedge,

Lifting quarters of rounds
　　covered with ants,
　"a living glove of ants upon my hand"
the poll of the sledge a bit peened over
so the wedge springs off and tumbles
　　ringing like high-pitched bells
　　　　into the complex duff of twigs
　　　　poison oak, bark, sawdust,
　　　　shards of logs,

And the sweat drips down.
　　Smell of crushed ants.
The lean and heave on the peavey
that breaks free the last of a bucked
　　three-foot round,
　　　　it lies flat on smashed oaklings—

Wedge and sledge, peavey and maul,
    little axe, canteen, piggyback can
    of saw-mix gas and oil for the chain,
knapsack of files and goggles and rags,

    All to gather the dead and the down.
        the young men throw splits on the piles
        bodies hardening, learning the pace
    and the smell of tools from this delve
        in the winter
            death-topple of elderly oak.
    Four cords.

True Night

Sheath of sleep in the black of the bed:
From outside this dream womb
Comes a clatter
Comes a clatter
And finally the mind rises up to a fact
Like a fish to a hook
A raccoon at the kitchen!
A falling of metal bowls,
        the clashing of jars,
        the avalanche of plates!
I snap alive to this ritual
Rise unsteady, find my feet,
Grab the stick, dash in the dark—
I'm a huge pounding demon
That roars at raccoons—
They whip round the corner,
A scratching sound tells me
        they've gone up a tree.

I stand at the base
Two young ones that perch on
Two dead stub limbs and
Peer down from both sides of the trunk:

Roar, roar, I roar
you awful raccoons, you wake me
up nights, you ravage
our kitchen

As I stay there then silent
The chill of the air on my nakedness
Starts off the skin
I am all alive to the night.
Bare foot shaping on gravel
Stick in the hand, forever.

Long streak of cloud giving way
To a milky thin light
Back of black pine bough,
The moon is still full,
Hillsides of Pine trees all
Whispering; crickets still cricketting
Faint in cold coves in the dark

I turn and walk slow
Back the path to the beds
With goosebumps and loose waving hair
In the night of milk-moonlit thin cloud glow
And black rustling pines
I feel like a dandelion head
Gone to seed
About to be blown all away
Or a sea anemone open and waving in
cool pearly water.

Fifty years old.
I still spend my time
Screwing nuts down on bolts.

At the shadow pool,
Children are sleeping,
And a lover I've lived with for years,
True night.
One cannot stay too long awake
In this dark

Dusty feet, hair tangling,
I stoop and slip back to the
Sheath, for the sleep I still need,
For the waking that comes
Every day

With the dawn.

PART TWO

Little Songs for Gaia

o

across salt marshes north of
San Francisco Bay
cloud soft grays
blues little fuzzies
illusion structures—pale blue of the edge,
    sky behind,

hawk dipping and circling
over salt marsh

ah, this slow-paced
system of systems, whirling and turning

a five-thousand-year span
    about all that a human can figure,

grasshopper man in his car driving through.

o

Look out over
This great world
Where you just might walk
As far as the farthest rim

There's a spring, there
By an oak, on a dry grass slope,
Drink.   Suck deep.

And the world goes on

o

The manzanita succession story—

Shady lady,
      makes the boys
            turn gray.

o

            trout-of-the-air, ouzel,
         bouncing, dipping, on a round rock
   round as the hump of snow-on-grass beside it
    between the icy banks, the running stream:
         and into running stream

            right in!

         you   fly

o

As the crickets' soft autumn hum
is to us,
so are we to the trees

as are they

to the rocks and the hills.

o

Awakened by the clock striking five
Already light,
I still see the dream
Three Corn Maidens in green
Green leaves, skirt, sleeves—
Walking by.
    I turned my eyes, knowing not to stare.

And wake thinking
I should have looked more
To see the way they were
Corn Maidens in green.
Green leaf face, too
Eyes turned aside.

But then I'm glad for once I knew
Not to look too much when
Really there.

    Or try to write it down.

o

The stylishness of winds and waves—
nets over nets of light
reflected off the bottom
nutcracker streaks over,
        hollering

Nature calls.
bodies of water
    tuned to the sky.

"Find a need and be filled by it."

                        o

Red-shafted
Flicker—
        sharp cool call

The smell of Sweet Birch blooms
Through the warm manzanita

And the soft raining-down
Invisible, crackling dry duff,

        of the droppings of oak-moth caterpillars.
        nibbling spring leaves

High in the oak limbs above.

                        o

Red hen on her side
    flips dust under her wing
    the free leg powerful,
        levering leaves and dirt,

In the afternoon manzanita shade
    her sisters too,
    this joy of dust and scrabble
        after morning's

Brisk scratch of bugs and weeds—
    they are all "seventeen"
    just into a life
        of egg-bearing pride,

May health, beauty,
    long life and wisdom
    come to the barnyard fowl,
        with humans to serve them:

World made for Red Hens.

                    o

        Hear bucks skirmishing in the night—

            the light, playful rattle
                of antlers
            in a circle of moonlight
        between the pond and the barn,
            and the dancing-pushing-
            stamping—and off running,

open the door to go out
to the chickencoop for eggs

○

Deep blue sea baby,
Deep blue sea.
        Ge, Gaia
Seed syllable, "ah!"

Whirl of the white clouds over blue-green land and seas
        bluegreen of bios   bow—curve—

Chuang-tzu says the Great Bird looking down,
        all he sees is
                blue . . .

Sand hills. blue of the land, green of the sky.
        looking outward
        half-moon in cloud;

Red soil—blue sky—white cloud—grainy granite,
                        and
Twenty thousand mountain miles of manzanita.
    Some beautiful tiny manzanita
    I saw a single, perfect, lovely,
        manzanita

                Ha.

○

One boy barefoot
    swinging madly
    in the driving rain
    I stand by the pond
    the hiss
Of rain into itself

o

Log trucks go by at four in the morning
    as we roll in our sleeping bags
        dreaming of health.
The log trucks remind us,
    as we think, dream and play

of the world that is carried away.

o

Steep cliff ledge, a pair of young raptors
    their hawklet–hood hanging
    over blue lake   over space

The flat green hayfields
    gleaming white *playa*   below

Hawks, eagles, and swallows
    nesting in holes between
                        layers of rock

Life of,
    sailing out over worlds up and down.
    blue mountain desert,
    cliff by a blue-green lake.

The Warner Range

o

Dead doe lying in the rain

    on the shoulder
    in the gravel

I see your stiff leg

    in the headlights
    by the roadside

Dead doe lying in the rain

o

I dreamed I was a god

last night. Melting the winter snows
with my warm breath. Bending low over
snowy mountains with the black sharp
scattered fir and pine, breathing,
"Haaaaaah"

o

Snowflakes slip into the pond
   no regrets.
Thin shoots of new-sprouted grass,
   it grows.
Two children learning Chinese checkers
And grownups sipping whiskey,
Spring evening snow.

o

THE FLICKERS

sharp clear call

THIS!

THIS!

THIS!

in the cool pine breeze

o

Hers was not a
Sheath.
It was
A
Quiver.

o

I am sorry I disturbed you.

I broke into your house last night
To use the library.
There were some things I had to look up;
A large book fell
            and knocked over others.
Afraid you'd wake and find me
and be truly alarmed
                        I left
Without picking up.

I got your name from the mailbox
As I fled, to write you and explain.

PART THREE

Nets

I

○

Walked Two Days in Snow, Then
It Cleared for Five

Saw a sleek gray bullet-body, underwater,
    hindfeet kicking, bubbles trailing,
    shoot under bushes on the bank;

A tawny critter on the gravel bar—
    first morning sunlight, lay down, ears up,
    watch us from afar.

And two broad graceful dark brown leaf-eaters with
    humped shoulders, flopping ears, long-legged,
    cross the creekbed and enter the woods.

A white and black bird soars up with a fish
    in its claws.

A hawk swings low over slough and marsh, cinnamon
    and gold, drops out of sight

A furred one with flat tail hung floating
    far from shore, tiny green wavelets, waiting;

And I saw: the turn of the head, the glance of the eye,
  each gesture, each lift and stamp

Of your high-arched feet.

IX, '74, Thoroughfare Meadow, Upper
  Yellowstone River

Geese Gone Beyond

In the cedar canoe gliding and paddling
on mirror-smooth lake;
    a carpet of canada geese
afloat on the water
who talk first noisy   then murmur

we stop paddling, let drift.
yellow larch on the shores
morning chill, mist off the
cold gentle mountains beyond

I kneel in the bow
in *seiza*, like tea-ceremony
    or watching a Nō play
kneeling, legs aching, silent.

One goose breaks and flies up.

    a rumble of dripping water
    beating wings
    full honking sky,

A touch across,
      the trigger,

The one who is the first to feel to go.

X, 79, Seeley Lake, Montana

○

Three Deer One Coyote Running
in the Snow

First three deer bounding
and then coyote streaks right after
            tail   *flat out*

I stand dumb a while   two seconds
blankly black-and-white of trees and snow

        Coyote's back!
        good coat, fluffy tail,
sees me: quickly gone.

        Later:
I walk through where they ran

to study how that news all got put down.

○

White Sticky

Glancing up through oaks
    dry leaves still hanging on,
    some tilt
    and airy wobble down, dry settles.
Pale early sun,
    standing in damp leaf ground
    pine needles, by dirt road,
    holding Gen's hand,
    waiting for his ride to school.

We talk about mushrooms.
This year was good
    but most got eaten by the worms.
There, under manzanita, more white stickies.
Can't find the bookname—
    glowing white and gooey cap,
    an unknown
    that we call "White Sticky" which is good
    as any name.

He goes off in Mike's old car to school,
    I walk back to the house
    try once more the mushroom book.

(*Hygrophorus?*)

Old Pond

Blue mountain white snow gleam
Through pine bulk and slender needle-sprays;
    little hemlock half in shade,
    ragged rocky skyline,

    single clear flat nuthatch call:
    down from the treetrunks

    up through time.

At Five Lakes Basin's
Biggest little lake
    after all day scrambling on the peaks,
    a naked bug
    with a white body and brown hair

    dives in the water,

Splash!

○

24:IV:40075, 3:30 PM,
n. of Coaldale, Nevada,
A Glimpse through a Break
in the Storm of the Summit
of the White Mountains

O Mother Gaia

sky   cloud   gate   milk   snow

wind-void-word

I bow in roadside gravel

I: VI: 40077

June 1, 1977
the earth goes on
a 40,000 yr cycle.

Ceanothus blossoms
   and the radiator boiling
      smells of spring

Fat rear haunches
   toes, tail,
   half a mouse
      at the door at dawn.
         our loving cat.

Setting sugar water
   feeder jars for bees out—
      hum of mosquitoes at dusk.

This year, the third
   of the bullfrog,
   he rarely speaks.
      Is it drouth and low water
       or age?

Kid coming out of the outhouse
　　　　at dusk in pajamas
　　　　　　　　still tucking them in,
　　　　　　　　　　　　"how many eggs?"

Last night, the first time,
　　　　raccoons opened
　　　　the refrigerator.
　　　　　　　　You can't slow down
　　　　　　　　　　　　progress.

"Aphids giving birth
　　　　to ninety live babies
　　　　　　　　a day."

II

The Grand Entry

The many American flags
Whip around on horseback,
Carried by cowgirls.
          the whirling lights of pleasure rides,
          the slow whine of an ambulance.

Two men on horseback roping head and leg of a calf:
Held immobile, from each end,
          a frieze;
          the crowd's applause;
          released, and scamper off.

Grassland biome technicians.
More spirit than those alluvial delta
High biomass priest-accountants
Who invented writing—

The announcer speaks again of the flag.
          the flag's like a steak: cowboys
          are solar energy-
          grass-to-protein
          conversion-magic priests!

Hamburger offerings all over America
Red, white,
and Blue.

> *Year of the bicentennial,*
> *Nevada County Fair rodeo*

o

Under the Sign of Toki's

Is this Palo Alto?
"No, Wisconsin."
    so gentle—distant older woman's voice—
                faint accent—Swede?
"Where are you?"   "This is Wisconsin."
Area code was wrong.
            what stream sipped from
            together in another life, to touch base
            ten seconds here in this?

        Toki's
    snack bar
    juice bar
        ice
    worms

And the operators
Keep asking me what do I want?
Sacramento, San Diego, Indiana, Ohio
    as I stand here with lists and letters,

outside, cold feet in the slush,
at the pay phone
(my office)

phone truck comes and takes coins while we talk
about art in LA
    under the ice sign
    next to the high way
talking,   ice   worms

    And snow
falls off the limbs
down my notebook
down into my neck
        drip drip
    red brick   iron doors   stone walls
old town run down
        at Toki's
          ice
      worms

The year I served as
chair for the California
Arts Council without a
phone at home and
twelve miles from the
pay phone next to
Toki's Okinawan Noodle
and Bait Shop

○

Talking Late with the Governor about the Budget

for Jerry Brown

Entering the midnight
Halls of the capitol,
Iron carts full of printed bills
Filling life with rules,

At the end of many chambers
Alone in a large tan room
The Governor sits, without dinner.
Scanning the hills of laws—budgets—codes—
In this land of twenty million
From desert to ocean.

Till the oil runs out
There's no end in sight.
Outside, his car waits with driver
Alone, engine idling.
The great pines on the Capitol grounds
Are less than a century old.

Two A.M.,
We walk to the street
Tired of the effort

Of thinking about "the People."
The half-moon travels west
In the elegant company
Of Jupiter and Aldebaran,

And east, over the Sierra,
Far flashes of lightning—
Is it raining tonight at home?

○

"He Shot Arrows, But Not
at Birds Perching"
Lun yü, VII, 26

The Governor came to visit in the mountains
    we cleaned the house and raked the yard that day.
He'd been east and hadn't slept much
    so napped all afternoon back in the shade.

Young trees and chickens must be tended
    I sprayed apples, and took water to the hens.
Next day we read the papers, spoke of farming,
    of oil, and what would happen to the cars.

And then beside the pond we started laughing,
    got the quiver and bow and strung the bow.
Arrow after arrow flashing
    hissing under pines in summer breeze

Striking deep in straw bales by the barn.

Summer, '76

○

Arts Councils

for Jacques Barzaghi

Because there is no art
There are artists

Because there are no artists
We need money

Because there is no money
We give

Because there is no we
There is art

What Have I Learned

What have I learned but
the proper use for several tools?

The moments
between hard pleasant tasks

To sit silent, drink wine,
and think my own kind
of dry crusty thoughts.

    —the first Calochortus flowers
    and in all the land,
        it's spring.
    I point them out:
    the yellow petals, the golden hairs,
        to Gen.

Seeing in silence:
never the same twice,
but when you get it right,

    you pass it on.

III

III

○

A Maul for Bill and
Cindy's Wedding

Swung from the toes out,
Belly-breath riding on the knuckles,
The ten-pound maul lifts up,
Sails in an arc overhead,
And then lifts *you*!

It floats, you float,
For an instant of clear far sight—
Eye on the crack in the end-grain
Angle of the oak round
Stood up to wait to be split.

The maul falls—with a sigh—the wood
Claps apart
          and lies twain—
In a wink. As the maul
Splits all, may

You two stay together.

○

Alaska

Frozen mist sheets low along the ground
    but outside town, at Gold Stream Vale
    forty below zero in the sun, stamp feet,
    chilled people in thick clothes,

Read what somebody sprayed on the yard-wide
    elevated tube, the shining pipe
    the heated crude oil travels,

  "Where will it all end?"

Drive back to stuffy rooms:
    lawyers, teachers, plant ecologists,
    energy visionaries, peoples' land managers
    cross minds

And then fly on to other towns
    dozing in planes
    the mountains

Soaring higher yet, and quite awake.

○

Dillingham, Alaska, the Willow Tree Bar

Drills chatter full of mud and compressed air
all across the globe,
    low-ceilinged bars, we hear the same new songs

All the new songs.
In the working bars of the world.
After you done drive Cat. After the truck
        went home.
        Caribou slip,
        front legs folded first
        under the warm oil pipeline
        set four feet off the ground—

On the wood floor, glass in hand,
        laugh and cuss with
        somebody else's wife.
        Texans, Hawaiians, Eskimos,
        Filipinos, Workers, always
        on the edge of a brawl—
        In the bars of the world.
        Hearing those same new songs
                in Abadan,

       Naples, Galveston, Darwin, Fairbanks,
        White or brown,
Drinking it down,

the pain
of the work
of wrecking the world.

○

Removing the Plate of the Pump
on the Hydraulic System
of the Backhoe

for Burt Hybart

Through mud, fouled nuts, black grime
it opens, a gleam of spotless steel
machined-fit perfect
swirl of intake and output
relentless clarity
at the heart
of work.

○

Glamor

A man who failed to master his Ally correctly
    when young, and was out seeking power,

so heard there were "white people" and left
    his own to go there,

and became infected with greed, went home
    with trade goods, they saw he was crazy.

Greedy, and crazy, the relatives should kill
    such a man, but this time no one did.

Crazy and greedy, he lives on. To the damage
    of his people.
Civilization spreads: among people who are generous,
    who know nothing of "ownership,"
    like a disease. Like taking poison.

    A glamorous disease
    a dazzling poison

    "overkill."

○

Uluru Wild Fig Song

1

Soft earth turns straight up
curls out and away from its base
hard and red—a dome—five miles around
　　　　Ayers Rock, Uluru,

we push through grasses, vines, bushes
along the damp earth wash-off watershed margin
　　　where vertical rock dives
　　　　into level sand,

Clustering chittering zebra finches on the
　　　　　bone-white twigs,
red-eyed pink-foot little dove,

push on, into caves of overhangs,
painted red circles in circles,
black splayed-out human bodies,
painted lizards, wavy lines.

skip across sandy peels of clean bent bedrock
stop for lunch and there's a native fig tree

heavy-clustered, many ripe:
someone must have sat here, shat here
    long ago.

      2

Sit in the dust
 take the clothes off. feel it on the skin
 lay down. roll around
 run sand through your hair.
 nap an hour

 bird calls through dreams
    now
   you're clean.

sitting on red sand ground with a dog.
breeze blowing, full moon,
women singing over there—
men clapping sticks and singing here

   eating meaty bone,
   hold the dog off with one foot

   stickers & prickles in the sand—

clacking the boomerang beat,
   a long walk
   singing the land.

3

naked but decorated,
    scarred.
white ash   white clay,
scars on the chest.
lines of scars on the loin.
the scars: the gate,
    the path, the seal,
      the proof.

white-barred birds under the dark sky.

4

singing and drumming at the school
a blonde-haired black-skinned girl
    watching and same time teasing a friend
dress half untied, naked beneath,
    young breasts like the *mulpu*
      mushroom,
swelling up through sand.

      stiff wind close to the ground,
      trash lodged in the spinifex, the fence,
      the bottles, broken cars.

5

Sit down in the sand
    skin to the ground.
    a thousand miles of open gritty land

white cockatoo on a salt pan

hard wild fig on the tongue.

this wild fig song.

*Fall of 40081, Uluru, Amata, Fregon,
Papunya, Ilpili,* Austral.

IV

o

Money Goes Upstream

I am hearing people talk about reason
Higher consciousness, the unconscious,
    looking across the audience
    through the side door
    where hot sunshine blocks out
    a patch of tan grass and thorny buckbrush

There are people who do business within the law.
And others, who love speed, danger,
Tricks, who know how to
Twist arms, get fantastic wealth,
Hurt with heavy shoulders of power,
And then drink to it!
    they don't get caught.
    they *own* the law.
Is this reason? Or is it a dream.

I can smell the grass, feel the stones with bare feet
    though I sit here shod and clothed
    with all the people. That's my power.

And some odd force is in the world
Not a power
That seeks to own the source.
It dazzles and it slips us by,
It swims upstream.

o

Breasts

That which makes milk can't
         help but concentrate
Out of the food of the world,
Right up to the point
         where we suck it,
Poison,too

But the breast is a filter—
The poison stays there, in the flesh.
Heavy metals in traces
         deadly molecules hooked up in strings
         that men dreamed of;
Never found in the world til today.
         (in your bosom
         petrochemical complex
         astray)

So we celebrate breasts
We all love to kiss them
         —they're like philosophers!
Who hold back the bitter in mind
To let the more tasty

Wisdom slip through
        for the little ones.
        who can't take the poison so young.

The work that comes later
After child-raising
For the real self to be,
Is to then burn the poison away.
Flat breasts, tired bodies,
That will snap like old leather,
        tough enough
        for a few more good days,

And the glittering eyes,
Old mother,
Old father,
        are gay.

Old Rotting Tree Trunk Down

Winding grain
Of twisting outer spiral shell

Stubby broken limbs at angles
Peeled off outer layers askew;
A big rock
Locked in taproot clasp
Now lifted to the air;
Amber beads of ancient sap
In powdery cracks of red dry-rot
    fallen away
From the pitchy heartwood core.

Beautiful body we walk on:
Up and across to miss
   the wiry manzanita mat.
On a slope of rock and air,
Of breeze without cease—

  If "meditation on decay and rot cures lust"
  I'm hopeless:
  I delight in thought of fungus,

beetle larvae, stains
      that suck the life still
      from your old insides,

Under crystal sky.
And the woodpecker flash
    from tree to tree
    in a grove of your heirs
On the green-watered bench right there!

    Looking out at blue lakes,
    dripping snowpatch
        soaking glacial rubble,
    crumbling rocky cliffs and scree,

Corruption, decay, the sticky turnover—
Death into more of the
Life-death same,

    A quick life:
    and the long slow
    feeding that follows—
    the woodpecker's cry.

VII, '78, English Mountain

106

o

For a Fifty-Year-Old Woman in Stockholm

Your firm chin
   straight brow
      tilt of the head

Knees up in an easy squat
   your body shows how
You gave birth nine times:
The dent in the bones
      in the back of the pelvis
mother of us all,
      four thousand years dead.

          X, '82, The Bäckaskog woman, Stockholm
                Historic Museum

o

Old Woman Nature

Old Woman Nature
naturally has a bag of bones
    tucked away somewhere.
    a whole room full of bones!

A scattering of hair and cartilage
    bits in the woods.

A fox scat with hair and a tooth in it.
    a shellmound
        a bone flake in a streambank.

A purring cat, crunching
    the mouse head first,
        eating on down toward the tail—

The sweet old woman
    calmly gathering firewood in the
        moon . . .

Don't be shocked,
She's heating you some soup.

VII, '81, Seeing Ichikawa Ennosuke in
"Kurozuka"—"Demoness"—at the Kabuki-za
in Tokyo

○

The Canyon Wren

for James and Carol Katz

I look up at the cliffs
But we're swept on by   downriver
                                      the rafts
Wobble and slide over roils of water
        boulders shimmer
        under the arching stream
Rock walls straight up on both sides.
A hawk cuts across that narrow sky
                        hit by sun,

We paddle forward, backstroke, turn,
Spinning through eddies and waves
Stairsteps of churning whitewater.
        above the roar
        hear the song of a Canyon Wren.

A smooth stretch, drifting and resting.
Hear it again, delicate downward song

        ti ti   ti ti tee tee tee

Descending through ancient beds.
A single female mallard flies upstream—

Shooting the Hundred-Pace Rapids
Su Shih saw, for a moment,
  it all stand still
"I stare at the water:
  it moves with unspeakable slowness"

Dōgen, writing at midnight,

  "mountains flow

  "water is the palace of the dragon
  "it does not flow away.

We beach up at China Camp
Between piles of stone
Stacked there by black-haired miners,
  cook in the dark
  sleep all night long by the stream.

These songs that are here and gone,
Here and gone,
To purify our ears.

o

The Stanislaus River runs through Central Miwok country and
down to the San Joaquin valley. The twists and turns of the river,
the layering, swirling stone cliffs of the gorges are cut in nine-

million-year-old latites. For many seasons lovers of rocks and
water have danced in rafts and kayaks down this dragon-arm of the
high Sierra. Not long ago Jim Katz and friends, river runners all,
asked me to shoot the river with them, to see its face once more be-
fore it goes under the rising waters of the New Mellones Dam.
The song of the Canyon Wren stayed with us the whole voyage; at
China Camp, in the dark, I wrote this poem.

April, 40081, Stanislaus River, Camp 9 to
Parrott's Ferry

○

For All

Ah to be alive
        on a mid–September morn
        fording a stream
        barefoot, pants rolled up,
        holding boots, pack on,
        sunshine, ice in the shallows,
        northern rockies.

Rustle and shimmer of icy creek waters
stones turn underfoot, small and hard as toes
        cold nose dripping
        singing inside
        creek music, heart music,
        smell of sun on gravel.

        I pledge allegiance

I pledge allegiance to the soil
        of Turtle Island,
and to the beings who thereon dwell

one ecosystem
in diversity
under the sun
With joyful interpenetration for all.

Design by David Bullen
Typeset in Mergenthaler Bembo
by Wilsted & Taylor
Printed by Maple-Vail
on acid-free paper